Average Jane Seeking an Average Joe

Average Jane Seeking
an Average Joe

Sandra B. Drosian

ISBN : 1-4196-3489-5

To order additional copies, please contact us.
BookSurge, LLC
www.booksurge.com
1-866-308-6235
orders@booksurge.com

Average Jane Seeking an Average Joe

Acknowledgements

This is dedicated to all of my single friends as well as married friends who have supported me and stood strong through the good times and the bad. There are so many of you that it would be unfair to mention you by name in case my depleting memory escapes me and I should overlook someone. You know who you are and you are forever in my thoughts.

You truly don't know who your best friends are until you think you are standing alone and that one friend is there to hold you up and give you encouragement and a hug when you need it most. Viv you are and always will be that friend and I will never forget your caring ways. You are the best.

Thank you and eternal love to my sons Richard and Ryan who have worried about me from time to time, not really understanding the different phases that I was experiencing, continuing to respect me and my space and to be there if I asked. A Mom couldn't ask for more and I thank God for giving me the privilege of bringing you both into this world.

Thanks to Francine, Eric and Gina for making my transition into your life so easy. Without you all, my final decision to take chances may have been different. I truly feel honored to be a part of your lives.

I should also thank the Joes who have come and gone and traveled down this path with me. Without you I would have nothing to write about.

This is especially dedicated to all of the Average Janes, Average Joes and all of the others who are looking for that special companion or partner, who have felt the disappointments and the rewards, enjoyed the good times along with the bad. And Congratulations and Good Luck to those of you who **have** finally found their soul mate.

Lastly but not least, I thank God for giving me the strength and encouragement as always. Without my faith I would never have found my way here, to my final destination.

Prologue

This was not originally planned to be a sequel to my previous publication, but after pondering the idea, I decided that yes, it could very well be a continuation to my story "True Desires". After my marriage ended in the year 1999, I was abruptly thrown into a new classification, "single", an identity I was not familiar with and one I never really experienced. This was not my choice but I had to make the best of it and see where it would lead me.

At first I thought it could be fun and exciting to begin dating at an age when my children are grown and not have the worrisome task of finding a responsible babysitter. I was mature and wise or at least I thought I was. I believed I would have no trouble at all meeting that perfect man. What I have learned five years later is quite the opposite. This experience for me has not been what I expected and if I knew what I know now, I perhaps would have taken a different path. I would have read books, maybe taken a course on being single, joined a monastery or safer yet, enrolled myself in a nunnery or convent.

I am writing this to share my experience, my highs and my extreme lows and to pass on my opinion and advice to those who through no choice of their own find themselves alone and in search of an Average Jane or Average Joe.

Introduction

Meet Jane, average middle-aged single mother of two grown boys, ages 19 and 24. Jane has been single now since the year 2000 and finally divorced for three. You see, I am Jane. I consider myself to be average, not a beauty queen, but attractive, not highly sophisticated but I'd like to think I am fairly intelligent, not a trend follower but try to keep in tune with the styles, no earned college degree, but the school of life, no high paying job, but a civil service employee who lives paycheck to paycheck.

I in no way regard myself to be an expert in today's world of dating but have found it to be a job in itself, a struggle, an adventure, an experience and sometimes a funny one at that. I never dated, always had one monogamous relationship that I clung to as if my life depended on it.

My first crush was Paul McCartney of the fab four from Liverpool England. I was 9 years old and it was love at first sight. At the same time, I also had a secret crush on my older cousin Clinton, but since I knew I could never marry him, I counted on Paul to fulfill this little girl dream of mine. I was going to marry him one day and whether he knew it or not, he was going to wait for me. This fantasy of becoming Mrs. Paul McCartney continued I believe until I was about 12. My next crush was on some boy I met in the schoolyard while swinging on the swings. I only remember his first name, Bruce, and when he looked at me, I felt something I didn't understand. It was a summer thing, two kids, teasing each other, taunting and competing to see who was better. That was it, the summer ended and I never saw him again.

Next was Tony, my Junior High School and Senior High School sweetheart. He was my first love. I'm not exactly sure how old we were when we met; I think it was 12 or 13. All I do know is that I was madly in love with him from the very start. I felt special being his girl and would fight any girl who tried to challenge that. It was silly really, a childish puppy love between two kids who didn't know any better. I looked up to him and depended on him to always be there for me and at the times he wasn't, I would literally fall apart. I loved this boy so very much. I loved the fact that I was his girl and no one would dare try to take me from him. I loved the attention he gave me but then there were times when the attention he gave me felt more like I was a possession. Not realizing it then, I probably acted the same towards him. I would hate it if I saw him talking to other girls and despised the times he was with his friends and not me. Again, we were much too young and didn't know enough to stand up for ourselves when we should have. Perhaps if we weren't so young it would have lasted longer, maybe even into marriage but at that particular time in our lives, we were too immature to exercise or understand the responsibility of commitments. We had many good times and memories that I will never forget but we also had differences that perhaps pushed me to wander outside my little box, into another world, a world without Tony. This is where my relationship with my husband came in.

Rich and I were 18, and what we found in each other, I'm not really sure. For me, it wasn't exactly a physical attraction, but it was the freedom to be who I wanted, independence I felt for the first time, the chance to more or less spread my wings and see what else life had out there for me. I was able to do things and not be questioned why. I could be me, the real Sandy. It was a best friend bond, a unity between two people seeking a connection with someone who would listen and not criticize. Whatever the actuality of it was, it lasted for 24 years. We married in 1976 and separated in the year 2000 after he disclosed his darkest secret to me, that he was gay.

After that awakening, I realized how little I knew, how much I needed to learn, how trusting I was of others and how stupid I felt. Here I was married to this man I thought I knew inside and out and I was blinded by the truth that was right there in front of me, literally spelled out in black and white in every which way. Blinded, is in all probability what I felt, but it is also a fact that I chose instead to ignore and go on in my marriage as if nothing was wrong. To this day, I still blame myself for not taking the initiative to end it sooner. My stubborn self-sacrificing ways forced me to think of everyone else in my life except for who mattered most....me, and of course my children who I thought at the time would be better with two parents in the household instead of one. I put my needs aside and continued to care and protect my kids from the sometimes traumatizing effects of divorce and what it can do to a child. I didn't want my children to experience the same emotions I went through. When I was young, divorce was such a taboo word, but now it's more common than marriage itself, almost as if it's expected. How sad for our children. How sad for today's society.

Anyhow, here I was now under this new "single" label and I hated it. Some people were envious of me, which I couldn't understand. All I knew was that I was alone and feared that this was my destiny. I wanted so desperately to find true love and to be loved, to feel all the things I lacked in my life and /or my marriage. All through my marriage I would often think of my "first love" and wonder if I had made the right decision. I would have bouts of guilt for even thinking of anyone else except my husband, for fear these thoughts that only God knew would be my curse forever. After my marriage ended I would torture myself occasionally with the *what ifs* and what if I had faced the red flags from the start? Would I have had the guts to go back to what meant so much to me in the first place?

I felt so inexperienced, like a teenage girl all over again. I had no knowledge of what real intimacy meant between a man and a woman, had never felt the things I read about in books or saw in movies or for that matter, on daytime soap operas. I had no knowledge of dating since I never really dated when I was younger. I went from my high school boyfriend of five years right into another relationship, with my now ex-husband.

Because of this insecurity of dating, I had even asked my ex-husband at one time to take me out to a singles bar just so I could see what I was in for. What I did see scared the living shit out me. Women my age and some even older wearing tight slinky outfits, either too short or too low cut and in my eyes and in my opinion, asking for trouble. And if it wasn't the clothing, it was the layers of makeup they had on. Did they really believe that this form of line filler was doing them justice? Did these women own mirrors and if they did, who did they see when they looked into it? Would I be one of these women one day?

For fear of ending up like one of those poor souls in the sixties mini skirt, I thought I would try my own method. I can't say it was all good, but it did give me something to write about. This uneasiness of being alone led me on one crazy journey that I will tell you about in as much detail as my conscious allows me. I have learned some hard lessons in a short period of time. At this moment, as I write this, I have already given in to my destiny, unless somewhere down the line, I'm shown differently.

Chapter One

Where do I begin?

Perhaps I should title this chapter, "Where do I end or when do I stop?" After a few years of recapturing memories of my journey, and editing here and there, I ought to tell you to stop right here and go on to the next chapter and come back to this one after you've finished reading this book.

Living in the wonderful world of computers made finding a date seem so much simpler. Of course now I think differently. The computer or the internet is like the root of all evils. If you don't respect it and use the information carefully and wisely, it can get you into shit load of trouble and unneeded pain. My vulnerability has forced me to learn so much in so little time. It's almost the end of another year, 2005 is right around the corner and after two major heartbreaks, I no longer have the energy or desire to meet my Joe. I'm tired and beat and have no more fuel to play this game anymore. I know its wrong of me to think this way but it's a game that I am not capable of playing.

Searching the Internet on the computer, there were so many online dating sites, so many places to look for single men, prospective and available and you could check them out just by a click of the mouse. You could read everything about them, from soup to nuts and if you were gullible like me, believe almost every word. That's where the disappointments come in, where eternal happiness soon turns sour, where your future dreams are nothing but dissuasion. My last venture ended this summer. I accepted failure and blamed myself and went into therapy in hopes of discovering exactly what I had been doing wrong. I decided I had to quit. It was over.

After some thinking however, instead of quitting all together, I decided to change my approach and take a different route. I joined some workshops and attended dinners geared for singles. The results were not what I expected but I have met some great people along the way, which has turned my discouragement of the dating life into an adventure of fun and discovery.

I'm not really looking for Joe anymore but instead, lasting friendship. If that Joe does happen to cross my path, then it will be by the hand of God and not by my fears of living the rest of my lifetime in solitude. And if this does happen and I do find eternal happiness, then I will more fully understand why I was pointed in this direction in the first place and why I had to go through the things I did.

So where do I begin? I am going to share with you the experiences, the wackiness and sometimes desperation that I have felt while in my pursuit of that special man. My intention is not to belittle anyone that I have met or be offensive in anyway. I would be the last one to say I am flawless, but let me tell you, I have met some characters out there, some amusing, some bizarre and two in particular who have turned my life upside down.

Being 50 years old doesn't keep me from dreaming or wishing on a star that my fantasy will come true. Who knows, perhaps by the time I finish this, there will be someone by my side to add a happily-ever-after ending.

Chapter Two

My first experience with Joe

After the separation from my husband in the year 2000, I had mixed emotions and some confusion as to how to go about fitting myself into the world of being single and available. I had never really dated in my life and was not really sure how or where to begin, especially at my age. Seeing that the computer was the most easiest and private way to start, that was where my first adventure began.

It was on "Love on AOL" that I posted my first profile in hopes of meeting my prince. It was fun at first and I got quite a few responses, some seeming ridiculous because of the age differences. It was somewhat flattering but at the same time, unbelievable that a kid my sons age would be responding to my profile. But then there were others, closer to my age, they came in all different sizes and shapes, many claiming astonishing qualities and backgrounds. It was here that I had contact with Joe #1.

We chatted online briefly and then advanced to the phone. Not really thinking things out, I gave him my phone number. *First rule*, never give your home phone number out! Thank goodness I have since then advanced to a cell phone. Our initial conversation seemed promising, especially upon hearing that he lived in a house, on waterfront property on the South Shore of Long Island. He never gave too much info about himself and our conversations were always short until I discovered that he lived with Mom and his younger brother. Realizing that this prince was not the one for me, I tried to ignore his constant phone calls and harassing emails. He was upset and accused that I had led him on, even though mind you, we had never met in person and had only spoken several times on the phone in a time span of about two weeks. Apparently I gave him the idea that we were exclusive, something more significant. Eventually the calls stopped and the angry emails ceased. So much for and good riddance Joe #1.

Feeling a little more confident and wiser, I returned to the AOL personals to resume my search. I was determined to meet my Average Joe and would not let a little crazy frighten me away.

A few more Joe's here and there, but never anything or anyone that caught my attention. There was one in particular however that did catch my eye, handsome and from what he described, secure and stable. We never really spoke, but instant messaged or IM'd each other on occasion. One afternoon while online, he IM'd me to ask if I wanted to meet for coffee. I was a little hesitant but told him I could meet him within the hour. It was then set, we would meet for coffee at a diner in Smithtown. I was just about ready to leave when he IM'd me once more asking if I was hot. HOT? What was he asking? What did he mean? I mean, yes, I was warm, it was a summer afternoon in August, but hot? Feeling somewhat foolish, I quickly shut off my computer as if he could see me standing there blushing and with a naïve and confused look on my face. Needless to say the meeting never took place. I did hear from him again, it was several weeks later when he sent me a message inquiring about my profile as if he never viewed it before. I reminded him that we had talked briefly before in the past....did he forget? He never replied so I guess that answered my question. Oh well, another Joe bites the Internet dust.

There were more every so often, and some with more baggage than I could handle. We all have problems and I admit mine are no better or less than the next person, but when a guy asks if you mind driving due to the fact that he has lost his license because of unpaid tickets or if you mind having young children around because his live-in girlfriend has abandoned hers, then its time to refocus and wonder just who and what is out there and posting on the internet in the first place. Then I look at myself...why am I posting on the Internet? Am I a loser or am I so desperately lonely that I will go to extremes to meet someone?

I tried instead to play it cool, ignoring men who did not fit my picture of a prince and did have some friendly conversations that never led to anything more. Then it happened, another Joe who went by the name of Louie. We conversed by email at first, then I decided I'd take another chance and try the phone. Actually, he was a very nice man, always giving me compliments, always boosting my ego and the self-image I had of myself. We exchanged photos and though he was not what I had imagined, I did not want to make judgment by some silly picture. After talking for a few weeks, we finally made a date to meet for coffee. It was a spur of the moment thing, he called one night and asked if I was available. After putting him off for so long, I figured I should go for it and see what happens.

Our coffee date was for 7 P.M. at a nearby Starbucks. It was a stormy night, thundering and lightning and hammering rain and I know I should have taken this as a sign from above, but ignoring those signs, I got in my car to see if this could be a possible prince. I arrived promptly at seven and looked around only to see an empty couch big enough for two. Getting my coffee, I sat and waited and waited and waited. Feeling a little uneasy and thinking that maybe I had been stood up, he suddenly appeared, my prince in shining or actually wet armor. He was wet from the rain and I had hoped, only shrunken from the dampness. He smiled, held out his hand and introduced himself. He resembled a well-known actor, whose name I will not mention here, not bad, but most definitely not my type. I watched as his smallish stature ordered coffee and wished I could run away or miraculously disappear at that moment. I felt disappointed and also guilty for immediately judging this man by his appearance.

As he approached the couch, I instantly placed my bag in between as if to put up a barrier. I tried to listen to him speak and ignore the constant rattle in my brain, "Run you bimbo, run!" I glanced at his eyes and the look on his face told me he was in love and if given the chance he would be in my lap. I wanted so desperately to think of an excuse to leave, but my brain was on inactive mode and all I could do was put on a false smile. Finally silence came and I realized it was my chance to call it a night. We stood and walked to the exit, Mr. Allen, I mean, Louie and I, and as I held out my hand to shake his, I mistakenly said something I should not have. "We should meet again, maybe for coffee again or a movie". What the hell was I saying? The words came out and I couldn't stop them. *Second rule*; if you don't want a second date, don't, I repeat don't suggest one!

It was too late and I suppose I did give him the wrong impression and the wrong message. He tried emailing me several times after that, and the wonderful plus thing about the Internet, is that you do not have to respond if you choose not to. My conscience got the better of me and I did respond eventually only to be told that I was NOT a nice person. I felt badly and only hoped that he would meet someone more his size and of course more honest than I had been.

I threw in my first towel and gave up on the AOL personals, but not for long.

Chapter Three

Meet Joe from Texas

Its now the year 2001, the summer has passed and being a bit lonely one night with no one to talk to, I searched the Internet for some chat sites. This in itself, can be dangerous if you are not careful, so many loonies out there, so many looking for a one-night stand via computer. Being somewhat cautious, I found a rather nice place, Moonlight Stroll, which after reading seem to have normal people, with normal lives. After browsing and reading about some of the members, I decided to post a profile about myself. I wasn't intent on looking for romance, but was looking for friends or pen pals and just everyday people like you and I that I could talk to. As quickly as I posted information about myself, I forgot about it, until several months later when I got an email out of the blue from a man who called himself Das Halten. This was my next experience with an Average Joe or whom I thought was average.

It was right after New Years Day, I had just promised and posted my resolution to myself for the year 2002. I was not going to search for my prince anymore but instead concentrate more on me and developing myself either financially or intellectually. I really felt I needed to work on these things in order to reach my new goals. Then it came, an email, simple and brief from this Joe of Houston Texas. He sounded harmless and because I do have friends from many places in the United States and he found my profile on Moonlight Stroll, I didn't see anything wrong in replying. This reply led to many more emails, then chatting online and then very long phone conversations, which became fun and very intriguing. Cowboy Joe was interesting and told me stories that were unbelievable. He spoke of places he visited, the languages he spoke, things he had experienced, activities that he was involved in, the family he had and the place he lived. At first he was a good friend, told me I could call him anytime but then our conversations became more intense, more personal and we were becoming more involved. I became so entranced that I couldn't wait to meet him in person.

We had planned our first meeting, he was coming up to visit me, but then at the last moment, there was a problem and he had to cancel. My disappointment was overwhelming and then an idea came to me, a crazy idea. Why not fly down there instead? I called him and asked him what he thought. I suppose he wanted to meet me just as much because he happily approved of my spur of the moment thought. It was agreed and set. After making arrangements at work for a few days off and spending my hard earned dollars for a last minute ticket, I excitedly packed my bags while caring friends and family tried to talk me out of this wild escapade. My mind was made up however, and no one could change what I was planning to do. I had to meet my cowboy, my prince charming in rawhide, boots and spurs that jingled jangled.

My fear of flying did not prevent me from going either. My endless prayers in the sky kept me glued to my seat as I dreamed in anticipation of looking into his green eyes for the first time. My nerves or instincts never told me to run, instead my heart told me to go forward and see what was ahead. This was something that had come to me when I least expected it and I took this as a sign from God, an opportunity to experience something totally new.

After landing, I looked around for my Southern Joe, no familiar face, no one who resembled the picture I had seen. As a matter of fact, the whole Texas thing was completely different than what I had imagined. Like projected in movies of the West, I expected to see real cowboys with cowboy hats, maybe riding horses instead of driving cars, but it was just like New York except that the pace was a little slower, the English a little more drawn out and the temperature for a winter season was warm and a bit humid. Then I saw him, the Average Joe from Texas. He was not at all what I expected, not extremely handsome, but also not entirely bad looking, not in great physical shape, but not obese in any way. He had great eyes like he described and a nice smile and his voice was exactly what I grew to love on the phone.

We drove in a well-worn Toyota truck, an hour away from the city of Houston, to a quaint little town called Livingston. We pulled up to a small trailer located in the RV park that he managed full time, where we spent the next few days together, getting to know each other, and me, getting to experience a life so different from my own. He treated me respectfully, showered me with kindness and for once I felt like a "purdy" lady. It was thoroughly enjoyable and I hated for it to end.

It didn't end, at least not right away and lasted for another year and half. In that time, I fell in love, not just with my prince from the South, but with his children, grandchildren, and this seemingly easier lifestyle and the state of Texas. With his words to take care of me and support me, and his sweet talk and caring ways, and for a woman in her forties, how could I turn away? The romance however only lasted for the first five months or so, and then it was downhill the remainder of the time. His job, his great pension and medical benefits, his past career and college education, his horses, cattle and the family ranch, the dreams we talked about together, getting married and buying a home, living happily ever after, were just words, words he used to engulf me in his game or maybe more precisely, his fantasy. Maybe he sensed that I was onto him, but his personality would change, like Jekyll and Hyde, from nice Joe to extremely cranky Joe, from hot to cold in a matter of seconds, sometimes not even remembering what he had said previously. At first he made me think I was being forgetful and at times, I really thought I was the one going crazy, but looking back, I think there was a possibility that he had some type of personality disorder. His words turned into lies and who he was, was just a blown up picture of who he really wanted to be, and me, wanting my fairy tale dream to never end, ignored the signs and red flags and tried to make it last.

He turned out to be a pathological liar, using alias names, with a trail of fraud behind him and even though I went along with his lies and even at times lent him money fully aware that I would never get it back, I tried to understand why he would deceive me knowing what I had been through in the past. I truly believed that he loved me and that he would never hurt me, but on my last visit to Texas to help him celebrate his 50th birthday, walls came tumbling down around me once again, the walls that I tried to hold up.

Like my marriage, I put myself in denial, I knew deep in my heart that for the past several months something was going on, something was not right. His calls came less, he was away more always giving excuses that he had to travel on business, he was harder to reach and he made himself less available to me. When I flew down there in June for his birthday, I overheard him talking to another woman on the phone. I should have known because of the miles between us, chances of him hooking up with another Jane was a great possibility, but like they say, love is blind or at least it made me blind for the time. I was hurt and my female ego was shot to pieces. What was so ironic about his new find, was that he met her on the same site he found me, Moonlight Stroll. He told this woman newer lies about himself, using yet a another name and not the Das Halten he used with me....this time he was Duke! I know he admired John Wayne, but this was ridiculous.

With some persuasion from his family, I ended up speaking to this woman and telling her the truth about her Duke. I felt terrible for shattering her world and stopping his, but I couldn't let him break another heart or take advantage of another vulnerable woman looking for love. I also contacted the website that he got our names from and explained to them the depth of his lies.

In the end, I don't think it was really so much the other woman. That in itself I could deal with, but it was the fact that he had fooled me along with his new Jane. His lies were out of control, he was in the process of fraudulently changing his name and moving away to be with her. He was convinced that he could get away with it, until I blew his cover. It ended up disastrous and his worried and angry family confronted him and tried to reach out to help, help that he claimed he didn't need. Unfortunately his mental unstableness will never allow him to find true happiness.

All of this was traumatic for me at first because I wanted to believe every word that he said, wanted to give him the benefit of the doubt, but in the long run it was for the best. This average Joe from Texas turned into another lesson in life, another experience with dating and feelings of love. The one positive aspect of the whole ordeal was that I have continued my friendship with his children and family and I did get to travel to a great state.

Though close friends and family swore they would kick his Southern ass way up North, I can't blame him completely for the way things ended. He never twisted my arm to fly down there, he didn't chain me to his side, and I had every opportunity to forget about him. It was my own foolish stubbornness and desire to have someone in my life, someone I could share my dreams with that kept me going back for more.

After all that happened and after my anger subsided, I wrote him again to offer support and friendship if he ever needed it. I think he really did love me at one time or else he would not have introduced me to his family and he would not have taken that chance of having himself exposed. He was far from stupid and had to know that eventually the truth would come out and I would find out who he really was.

So much for what I thought was true love, so much for riding off into the Texas sunset and so much for this Average cowboy Joe. *Third rule,* don't fall for liars, if it sounds too good to be true, that's exactly what it is.... too good to be true!

Chapter Four

Back in the saddle again...

I n that year and a half, I was totally dedicated to my cowboy in Texas, never tempted to look elsewhere, never had a desire for more in a relationship. I was sincerely content knowing that one day we would be together forever, but completely frustrated that we didn't see each other as much as I myself needed. I admit, there is a selfish side of me that wants the company of a man 24/7. I've had too many lonely nights, too many days of doing things by myself and making decisions alone. My kids are grown and I have the opportunity now to focus all of my attention on that special guy and expressing my love and total devotion.

Now that the Texas dream was over, I had to get myself back into the saddle once again. I felt I tried the long-distance thing and saw how difficult and frustrating it could be; now I had to get back to basics and stick with the locals. During the Texas fling, I had hid the profiles I had posted on many online dating sights, but now that it was over, I had to get to work updating and "un-hiding" them all. Some of the well-known dating services online were Friendfinder, Matchmaker, American Singles, Yahoo Personals and the infamous Match.com. All of these services are great if you have a full membership, simply meaning, you then have the ability to contact men you may be interested in. If you don't pay, you can't play...all you are is an ad with a picture, it's as simple as that. With this is in mind, I reinstated my membership with Friendfinder and Match.com.

Friendfinder didn't do much for me, but Match.com, perhaps because I think it is the most popular online dating service, gave me more choices and found me more "mutual" matches. I met quite a few men, some extremely nice, but since in the past I found myself settling for less, I decided to reach for the stars, and look for Prince Charming with a Gates or Trump bank account. What is that old saying? First time is for love, second time is for money? Ok, let's shoot for the money.

This type of search didn't last long; those guys weren't interested in me and me in them. Their lifestyles were too extravagant, too fast paced, and much too advanced for me. Their profiles talked of many homes and countless vacations. Their free time was spent golfing, playing tennis, scuba diving, skiing, cruising on either their boats or motorcycles, and numerous other hobbies. If a man did this much in his life, then how the heck would he have time for a woman? I can't pretend to be someone I'm not, therefore felt I could never fit in, so I quickly changed my specifics and reverted back to me, Average Jane looking once again for that Average Joe. Forget the money Sandy, look for that plain old fashioned love.

Chapter Five

More Joe's, more discouragement...

So here I am, its mid summer of 2003 and I'm on my quest. Where is he? Where is he hiding? My Texas relationship still fresh and still aching a bit, I plunge right in and begin "winking" and chatting with a few new Joe's. Winking is a way of letting someone know that you may be interested; the only downfall is it can also give you a feeling of rejection when the wink is not acknowledged or reciprocated. This all sounds entirely ridiculous to someone on the outside that isn't familiar with the "single" thing, but this is the way it is believe it or not. It's the easiest way of letting someone know that there may be a possible attraction without ever meeting them, by first chatting or exchanging emails. In this way, you can get some introduction to their personality and perhaps a sense of the type of person they are. With my previous experience of Joe's looking for HOT babes, Joe's looking for a quick fling and Joe's who lie, I now find myself being overly cautious.

I winked at an average looking Joe who in turn contacted me while online. We chatted very briefly and quickly advanced to the cell phone. He sounded sincere on the phone and harmless at that, so we made an "appointment" to meet at *my* Starbucks. Our meeting went well. He was to some extent interesting and I found it amusing that he wore a ring with the super "S" insignia. We talked a bit about his life and his family then it was my turn. This is where my hurt ego surfaced. I thought I could hold it all together but I think I gave him a true sense of the pain I still carried since the Texas breakup. He kept asking me about that relationship and what it was that kept me going back for more and as I tried to find answers deep in my heart, the tears kept welling up in my eyes. Now that I'm totally embarrassed because my bruised ego is open and in view of this complete stranger, I just want to jump in my car and rush home to curl up in my bed and cry. Upon leaving, he gave me a polite kiss on my cheek, and still feeling violated emotionally, I had hoped to never hear from him again. Truthfully, I felt no attraction to him at all, and because of my sudden show of tears, thought maybe I jumped into the online dating thing too quickly.

He did contact me again after that, but after evaluating our meeting and the things we talked about, I felt he would never understand the type of person I was, never understand how my heart ticks. Goodbye "Super" Joe.

Next is the arrival of "Anti-war" Joe. I chose the anti-war label, because through our chatting and online conversations, I discovered he was an artist, and portrayed his feelings against war visually through art. We only exchanged emails for a couple of weeks, teasing here and there and then the usual advancement to the phone. We had a lot of fun, joking and making each other laugh, and then sharing some serious conversations as well. During this time, I didn't have a picture of him and relied only on my imagination. He had a very sexy voice and I felt he enjoyed listening to the silly things I talked about and I enjoyed listening to him as well. We finally decided to meet in person, though, after Super Joe, I was so afraid that I would fall apart once again.

By this time, I thought seriously of asking for commission at Starbucks, but figured the young people behind the counter would look at me as though I was crazy, and in all probable fact, I was. Instead of making this foolish request, I ordered my coffee and sat at a small table with a book and waited patiently and nervously for the sexy voice on the phone. He arrived, really not a bad looking man at all, except that I felt he was still stuck in the 60's or 70's era. His hair was long, neatly kept in a ponytail, the only bad fault that I knew I could not handle was his smoking.

Maybe he was nervous, but he smoked continuously which completely turned me off. I really liked this guy, really thought maybe I could overlook this bad habit, but after thinking it over, I knew it would be so unfair of me to expect him to change if we ever did get involved and because I expected someone to accept me for who I am, I had to do the same. Good-bye Anti-war Joe. Upon leaving, I kissed him politely on the cheek and cried once again on my way home wondering if the average Joe even existed.

Back to the drawing board or rather back to the Internet. More Joes, more discouragement, more possible dates that never take place, it's the end of the summer and I want to run away. And I did. My stepbrother and his lovely wife offered my sister and I a weekend getaway to their beautiful home in the Bahaman Islands. Loving the beach and the warm weather immensely, I took them up on it and who knew...perhaps there was an Average Tropical Joe somewhere?

Chapter Six

Hands-on Joe

The Tropical Island Joe didn't exist either. After arriving on this beautiful island, the only action I found was an unexpected slap on my derrière from my brother's family friend as I climbed a staircase to the sunroom in their beach house. This alarming surprise quickly changed my normally friendly behavior, to doing everything possible to avoid any contact with this particular gentleman. To prevent any embarrassment I will not mention his name, but instead of taking his action upon my butt as a personal one, I have just convinced myself that he is one of the many men who have a difficult time keeping their hands to themselves. If he was an old friend or for that matter a boyfriend, I would in no way be offended by the swiftness of his hand, but having only just met him, the hands-on contact caught me completely off guard.

The island was beautiful, the weather magnificent and the search for that single eligible bachelor was to no avail. The only men sighted were the residents of the island who already had that lady in waiting or a permanent partner and the employed workers who commuted each day to this paradise island. So instead of finding discouragement, I vowed to sit back and take in the sun, enjoy the peace of the ocean and to run and hide when the hands-on gent appeared.

After three days of a relaxing getaway, we headed back to reality, my single sister and I. Arriving back in New York with a clear and refreshed mind, I thought about some new tactics, maybe some original catch phrase, and a revamped profile to catch the eye of a looker. My quest was not over, I would not give up, I was determined to find the man of my dreams.

Chapter Seven

A New Profile

Of all the online dating sights, choosing one or two was turning out to be more of a challenge than the motive itself. Offers for 30-day free trials, options to view eligible members, questionnaires to assist in finding that perfect match, downloading /uploading pictures, different membership packages, choices to chat online or stay hidden so that others cannot see you, all of these things were becoming more of a nuisance than anything else. What at first seemed like the easiest and safest way to meet someone was turning into a job, almost like an employer looking for the right employee to fill the vacant position. It got to the point where I couldn't keep track of all of the dating sites I had profiles on. This and the inability to remember my passwords to access these sites, forced me to choose and commit to only one dating site. The one I chose was Match.com. Being familiar with this one and knowing the credibility it had, I decided to update my present profile and see what kind of responses I would get.

First I needed to come up with an original opener or introduction line. Looking at the other profiles posted, they all seemed the same, all looking for the same thing. "Knight in Shining Armor", "Lady in search of Prince Charming", "I'm ready for you, are you ready for me?" Then it came to me, exactly who I am and exactly what I'm looking for, "Average Jane seeking an Average Joe". That was it, it was all I needed. To me it explained it all. I didn't want to meet the CEO of some growing company, didn't want to meet the guy with the six figure salary who has it all, does it all and wants a bosom buddy to do more with, I didn't want to meet a man who conveniently forgets his age and thinks he looks fifteen years younger.... I just wanted to meet someone who shares the same interests as me, someone who works hard like me, someone who is honest and sincere and who has no reason to exaggerate what life has given them so far. In other words, I don't want to play games, I'm a serious woman looking for a serious friendship, one that could easily blossom into something more.

Next was the location. Did I want to limit myself to a 10-mile radius or extend it to 20 miles or more and increase my chances of meeting someone in New Jersey or Connecticut? Did I really want to take another chance with a long distance relationship? And what age was I looking for? Did I want to stick to someone my own age or take a swing at meeting someone just a little bit younger? After watching an Oprah show not too long before, the topic being, "older women dating younger men" and seeing just how great these women looked, I decided, what the hell, lets go a little younger. I thought a range of 42 – 52 was playing it safe. Then I had to answer some simple questions, list likes and dislikes, turn ons and turn offs, and then describe myself and whom I'd like to meet.

Average Jane seeking an Average Joe

If I am meant to sell myself to you, the Average Joe, I would say simply that I am a single hard working Mom of 2 grown boys. I am attractive, take care of myself, am considerate of others, respectful of feelings, self-supportive, generous, sincere and trustworthy, loving and fun to be with and try not to take life so serious all of the time. I am not materialistic; enjoy the simple things in life; the beach, the sound of the waves crashing against the shore, a beautiful sunset or sunrise, a moonlit stroll, drives to nowhere, a roaring fireplace, a candlelit dinner and a glass of wine, cuddling and romance and a loving relationship with that average guy who is in search of his average woman. I am at a time in my life when I can enjoy all that I have missed, could you be looking for the same?

I'd like to meet a man who knows what he wants in life, a man who is strong, yet sensitive, cares about himself as well as others, is financially secure, completely honest and is a good communicator. Someone who can make me laugh, comfort me and love me for who I am. A guy who is ready for a relationship and knows that building one takes time and understanding by both partners. Love grows and life can be enjoyed with that special someone, could that someone be you?

So that was it, I saved it and sent it and waited patiently for the first Average Joe to respond.

Chapter Eight

Patiently waiting

While waiting for my new Joe's to respond, well meaning friends decided to set me up with a friend of theirs. A single man, with a similar situation like mine, a marriage that turned out to be full of denial and probably lies. We tried emailing each other few times but with no luck. We just couldn't get a conversation going which led me to think our meeting was just not meant to be, and then finally he made contact by phone. He sounded nice but still we did not get to talk at all or get to know each other a little before our first meeting. Except for what my well-meaning friends told me about him, I had no clue as to what type of person he was, what he looked like, where he lived or how ready he was for a friendship with me and I don't know how much he knew about me either.

At last the time came as I nervously waited for him to arrive. He picked me up for our first date, and like a gentleman, opened the car door for me and there on the seat was a beautiful bouquet of roses. How very sweet coming from someone I have never met. Again, it was to my infamous Starbucks where we tried to relax and exchange friendly conversation. He was very intent on listening to my tales but I felt as though I was stealing the limelight, nevertheless, we seemed so comfortable enough with each other that he suggested we take a ride down to a nearby marina where we could walk around and take in the summer night. The night went nicely as we talked but I noticed he kept bringing up my likes and dislikes that were listed on my profile. It seemed as though he was trying to fit himself into everything that I was looking for in a man. Then the night was over and he was driving me home. I was already feeling that we really had nothing in common except for the similarities in our ex-spouses but I wanted to give him the benefit of the doubt and not make judgment so quickly. We agreed to meet again the next day for dinner and a movie. We pulled up to my house and he walked me to the door and like a gentleman, gave me a gentle kiss. That was enough for me and I most definitely did not give him the impression that I wanted or expected more.

He called the next day in the afternoon and we made plans to meet again. He arrived on time, once again, a gentleman, opening and closing the door for me and oh how nice it felt to be treated like a lady. We went for dinner first and as we ate I realized that I was making a mistake. I felt no chemistry whatsoever and I even began finding myself getting a little defensive when we discussed my over abundant ways of caring for the people in my life. I think what turned me off the most was something he said about changing my ways. Here I was sitting with a man who I knew for less than 48 hours and already he was changing me. "This is who I am!" I wanted to scream at him, "I can't change the person I am". But I continued to eat my dinner and smile between bites and longed for the night to end. Afterwards we went to the movies and I wished then that I had told him I was suddenly ill, but feeling badly enough, I sat through it all.

The movie finally over, he drove me home as I silently tried to think of what to say. We pulled up in front of my house and I quickly opened the door without waiting for him to come around to my side. I knew he was walking right behind me as I turned around to say good night, he pushed his lips up against mine and tried to make it a romantic kiss, but I could only respond with the coldness that I felt. He said he would call me so we could plan another date.

I never felt so miserable about myself as I did then. Why did I agree to another date? Why couldn't I just tell him I didn't think it would work, that there was no connection between us?

What happened to open and honest Sandy? Instead I retreated to my room and my faithful friend, my computer, and sent him an email, the coward's way out. I explained that he did nothing wrong, that he did everything right, but that I didn't feel that we had anything in common therefore did not want to lead him on into thinking we could have more. I told him I would be happy to continue as friends if that was okay with him.

I never heard him from again. Poor Joe trying so hard to make a good impression and what did I do? I rejected his kindness and his advances. I still felt badly but knew that in time, he, like I had in the past, would just suck this up to an experience in dating.

Chapter Nine

Moody Joe

Back to Match, checking out all the available bachelors or would-be, could-be potentials. I decided to look outside my circle of mutual match-ups and see who was online in a 25-mile radius. One guy caught my eye immediately. He had the most gorgeous blue eyes that seemed to stare back at me through my computer monitor. I admit I flirted here, but I had to send him an email just to let him know that I adored his eyes, and to my surprise, he responded.

We didn't email each other in the usual way to get to know each other, but began by chatting online. He was 43, single, never married, currently out of work, residing temporarily with his sister and her family in Connecticut and the big shocker was that he had just recently moved here from Austin Texas. I couldn't believe it...another Texan!! What are the odds of that happening? He lived in Austin for several years and after being unemployed for almost a year, decided it would be best to move north, back to his hometown in Connecticut.

We had a lot of fun chatting and getting to know each other and in that time I discovered he had mood swings that fluctuated as much, and if not more than my own PMS. When he was down, he was horrible to communicate with. He would accuse me of not caring about his feelings, not showing enough compassion in regards to his circumstances and would get angry with me if I didn't start off each conversation by asking how he was. When I did ask how he was doing, he would get angry with me for asking too much or smothering him. Each time we spoke, I never knew what to expect. He didn't like to talk on the phone and very rarely called me, most of our conversations were by "instant messaging" each other online.

This went on for two months and in that time, we did meet in person and spend time with each other twice. The first time I met him was in Port Jefferson, when he came across the LI sound by ferry. He was a big guy, 6'2", clean-shaven, unlike his picture on Match, and looked more like a big teddy bear. Much to my surprise, he was quiet, and unlike the personality he displayed online. At times I found it hard to make conversation but did my best to find things to talk about. The second time we met he drove to my home from Connecticut. It was a nice meeting but here we are again and still there was that silence between us. We spent some time together and then he left.

What happened after that meeting is not too clear. All I recall is that he was extremely distraught about being unemployed, confused and worried as to what to do next and his horrific mood was more than I could handle. I tried being nice, tried being sympathetic and compassionate and tried being understanding, but nothing I did was good enough. We ended up arguing, my feelings were hurt and I retaliated with some harsh words. The bottom line was he was too self-consumed with his problems and his situation and really had no time for a relationship.

It was all for the best, I had two sons already and didn't need another one. Another lesson in dating? Another lesson in recognizing a personality dysfunction? Whatever it was, I came to the conclusion that two Texans were more than enough for me. Moody Joe, Austin Joe or "Hope You Get a Job Joe", this was not the Average Joe for me.

Chapter Ten

Here I go again

I was determined not to let Moody Joe deter me from finding my prince. He had to be out there somewhere, but just where was my biggest problem. I continued on my mission, and over the next few weeks I met a few more men. One in particular seemed very nice, friendly and though we never got to the point of meeting in person, I realized that he was not the Joe for me. He was a few years younger than I, had a young son who he spent much time with and the only fault I found was that all of our conversations centered around him. This was too much of a reminder of Moody Joe and I was glad that we never actually got to meet.

Then there was another man I began chatting with from Connecticut. He was ok; our conversations didn't go too far especially when I mentioned to him that I was writing a book about my dating experiences. I'm guessing there was more to his situation than he revealed because I never heard from him again. That should be a tip for future reference...looking for the truth? Just tell em' you're writing a book!

The online encounters continued with Fisherman Joe, Rodeo Joe, Security Guard Joe, Nascar Racing Joe and some that I lost track of. I never met any of these men in person, just had some conversations either online, by email or by phone. Some seemed friendly enough, but our interests were not the same so there was no point in pursuing any further.

There was one man however who caught my attention because I thought we had similar interests. He enjoyed sunrises and sunsets, enjoyed walks along the beach, holding hands and cuddling in front of a fireplace, and listed numerous adventures that he had already experienced. Wow! I was astonished. I sent him an email and kept my fingers crossed in hopes that he wasn't already spoken for. Almost immediately he responded and no, he wasn't currently involved with anyone. I felt as though my luck was changing. We emailed over the next couple of days and now because I was becoming such a pro at this thing, advanced to the phone. His voice sounded nice, he seemed interested in me and what I like to do for fun so we decided not to waste anymore time and planned on meeting in the morning at the local diner to chat more. No more Starbucks for me! It was table service this time, with not only coffee, but juice, scrambled eggs, bacon and buttered toast to top it off. This felt real and though I was nervous, I felt confident. The New Year had just begun and excitement stirred inside me that told me 2004 was going to be a good one...

It was a cold Sunday morning; the sun was shining bright and trying its hardest to warm the air. I pulled into the parking lot of the diner and still feeling energized and positive, walked proudly, head held high as I marched into the diner to meet my prince. There he was waiting at the doorway, bundled warmly, prepared for the current winter temperatures. He held out his hand, I extended mine for the prince's kiss, but instead we shook hands. A rush of disappointment overcame me as I expected someone a bit taller, perhaps a little younger looking. I cursed to myself, why are pictures so deceiving?

Ok, I thought, looks are not what its all about. It's about compatibility, fun and laughter, sharing, communication, *tall, dark and handsome*, honesty, chemistry, *tall dark and handsome*. Did I say that twice?

We did communicate nicely, he told me about his family fish store, about his current position as a Realtor, his son, his home on the lake, his experiences. He told me he was never married.

Stop! Should this be a red flag? Calm down girl, don't jump to any conclusions. Give the guy a chance for heavens sakes.

Finally our meeting was over, we sort of went Dutch and while he paid for the breakfast, I left the tip. He walked me to my car and asked if he could call me again. He really was nice and I needed to give him a chance and open myself to more opportunities. It was a mutual decision; he would call me during the week.

The following week was a blur to me, I didn't hear from him right away but he called on Thursday and asked if I'd like to go for dinner on Friday. I welcomed dinner and the chance to get to know this prospective Average Joe. I willingly gave him directions to my house and would expect him to arrive at approximately 7:30 pm.

Friday night arrives; he has called several times asking which street, what street, turn left, turn right? I wanted to scream into the phone, you work in Real Estate, how could you not know where you are but by now I'm standing outside on the edge of my driveway talking to him on my cell phone, giving him directions as I watch a car travel by slowly three or four times. He approaches my house once more, this time I'm ready to jump out in front of the vehicle to stop it, when he rolls down his window to ask directions. Doesn't he even remember what I look like? Hey you, Average Joe, it's me, your date, but instead I call out his name and graciously walk around to the passenger side of the car and get in. I'm cold and a little frustrated but then this quickly fades as he hands me some flowers. Oh gosh, how sweet and what a nice gesture for someone who has spent the last half hour standing outside in the brutal cold air giving Mr. Real Estate a tour of the neighborhood. Then I'm caught off guard when he asks me what I want to do. Did I misinterpret his offer for dinner, my mind still frozen from the outside air? His next words were something about a fireplace and wine. Not really thinking and not too quick, my naïve brain says, ok, that sounds nice. I had no idea what was on his agenda nor did I think I could be endangering myself. I'm 49 years old, what could possibly happen?

I think we drove to someplace in Patchogue though I'm not sure because it was very dark out and I couldn't make out the street signs. It seemed like we drove forever and I was totally lost. We turned up a dark road, lined with dimly lit houses, which reflected on an adjacent lake. Pulling into a graveled driveway the house I saw before me was far from what I estimated for someone who sold houses for a living. It was a cottage, probably a summer bungalow at one time and looking a bit dilapidated. I kept reassuring myself that it wasn't that bad, after all it is evening and hard to see without proper lighting.

I followed this Joe into his home, and knew right then that I had made a dreadful error. My instincts clicked in and told me to run, escape while I had the chance, but I had no idea where I was and the cold winter air ushered me inside. I imagined the headline in the local newspaper, "Missing Average Jane found.... Stupid Stupid Jane". I had to stop thinking like this.

The room was dark and brightened ever so slightly when he lit some candles. I carefully walked to the couch, only a few steps away and tried not to notice the look of unkemptness or specs of litter on the floor. He went into the kitchen area to wash a glass for the wine. Oh no! I wanted to scream, get me out of here! I calmly accepted the glass filled with wine as he pulled a snack table over and placed some wilted flowers on it, the same type of flowers he handed me in the car. "Oh God", I prayed to myself, "I am so sorry for being brainless, please get me home to my kids safely!" He attempted to light a fire to bring some kind of warmth to the room and then he sat on the couch near me as I sat on the edge with my coat on, prepared and ready to run away from my captor. He tried to make conversation, showing me the many layers of clothing he had on, talking about marriage, about his bedroom, again about his bedroom, about the warm bedroom, more about his freaking damn bedroom and then about what you do on the second date....second date! I thought this was the first date! Here I go again, I'm blaming myself, and I felt terrible that I had given this man the wrong idea about me. I suddenly felt very cheap, hungry because I had no dinner, unappreciative of the wilted grocery store flowers, obsessive compulsive because of the dirty wine glass, cold because of the lack of heat and how the hell could I be so incredibly dumb! I told him I was feeling uncomfortable and asked him to bring me home. Not giving up so easily and after some more suggestions, I guess he finally realized I wasn't there to please him, I was not his one night stand or some discounted date. I was a mature woman looking for some mature responsible dating and I was surely misled into thinking differently.

He drove me home, as I silently thanked my guardian angel for watching over me and swearing that this would never ever happen again. This was another experience in dating, one I will never forget and thankfully I can look back and laugh about it.

Another rule to remember, never go to a mans house expecting just wine and a roaring fireplace! And a word of advice to all you men out there, please clean your place before you invite a lady over.

Chapter Eleven

Every woman's worst nightmare

This chapter was the hardest for me to write, so hard in fact, that I deleted and added entries and then at one time, erased everything I had written. At the time I was angry, heartbroken and feeling deceived again, as in the past. Now looking back and where I am now, I will not even waste time going into the details involved in this affair. This Joe who I called BB, was dishonest from the beginning and the things I learned over the months that we dated should have been enough for me to tell him to take a hike. I got swept into a romantic whirlwind, his wining and dining and weekend getaways and fell for all of his rehearsed lines and in his case, lines he said to me and another girlfriend, word for word. That's right...another girlfriend, one he told me he was through with. I was betrayed by two people here, "BB" and the so-called ex-girlfriend "J".

When we began, I really thought I was being cautious enough, taking time and being careful not to get hurt again but after several weeks of seeing each other and feeling fairly sure that he was being sincere, I made the mistake of offering a spare toothbrush. This invitation turned into routine weekends and mid-week stay-overs. I won't deny that I didn't enjoy his company, but I should have realized so much more about him especially when I saw the picture of his ex-girlfriend on his dresser. He was aware that this bothered me, but instead of taking the picture and putting it away, he would just place something else in front of it. Red flags, neon blinking flags, for goodness sakes Sandy wake up!

He deceived me by telling me I could trust him and that he was here to stay. Let me repeat this "Here to stay"...that's the statement that got me the most. Needless to say, in the month of May after my birthday, I found out how much he was lying to me. Apparently he and his girlfriend "J" had this weird agreement between them, "don't ask, don't tell" and I became part of their cat and mouse game with each other.

There was so much more in between all of this, but at the point I am at now, he and this now past experience is not significant enough to write about. This is every woman's worst nightmare, a romantic liar. He lied to his wife, lied to J, lied to me and who knows how many more.

By the way, did I mention he was from Texas? Yep, another Texan. I don't mean to give Texas men a bad rap because I know there are some very nice ones out there, but unfortunately for me, I fell for the wrong cowboys.

To make this story short, BB moved back to Texas in November and promised me we could continue our friendship. He also told me things could change anytime and he could come back. More lies. As a matter of fact, I did hear from him a few more times after that but knew in my heart that I had to let it all go. Why was I torturing myself and allowing him to get his jollies and male ego on a high? I told him not to email or call me unless his Southern Belle J knew about it. Once a cheater always a cheater.

He once told me he was not worth it, and he was most definitely correct about that. She can have him because I know that I deserve much better. J gave me a warning at one time and if she ever reads this, here is my chance to pass on a suggestive warning to her. He referred to her once as "weight challenged". After getting to know BB, I realized he is happy when he has a pretty fit lady by his side. One last word of advice J... make sure you keep him on a short leash. When he drinks, he flirts and forgets and who knows where that can lead. Possibly a topless bar, a massage parlor or New York to visit a friend? Good luck J, you'll need it.

As for that toothbrush? It came in handy when cleaning the bathroom and getting to those hard to reach places around the commode.

Chapter Twelve

I'm through, no more for me!

After that relationship ended in May, I found myself seeking therapy. I was depressed and frustrated with myself. How could I be so stupid again? Most of all, what was I doing wrong? Was I trying too hard to meet someone? So many questions and no answers. Would a therapist be able to help me?

A close friend of mine suggested that I see a male therapist. I did and upon entering his office during my first visit, I announced that I hated men. What a horrible thing to say, but after all the trust I put in the men in my past, it was how I felt and I wasn't going to deny it. Every man in my life deceived me in some way, excluding my own sons of course. Those men I cared about only thought of themselves.

After many weeks and after evaluating myself once again, I discovered that I was co-dependent. What exactly did that mean for me? It meant that I go out of my way to please as if I am trying to win love or approval. I blame myself for the things that go wrong and defend the people who were responsible. I am an enabler, a forgiver and a martyr of my own doing. I am everyone's best friend except my own.

Thankfully my therapist turned out to be someone who I felt very comfortable talking to. I revealed and exposed things that I was not even aware of. I needed to do a lot of work with this psyche of Sandy. Besides some brain work, I got myself back into my exercise routine. Exercise was not only good for my body but helped me release some pent up stress. It helped me to relax and feel good about myself.

Meanwhile I had joined a Workshop for singles and attended dinners geared especially for singles. The workshops were great and I met some nice people who, like me, felt that life had in some way short-changed them. We are all good people looking for something that we can't find. The founder of this workshop explained how we needed to make lists and prioritize what we are looking for in a companion. After some thought the first thing on my list had to be honesty. I was lied to way too many times and had a bad habit of dismissing what I thought could be lies because I didn't think anyone would do this to me once they got to know me. I added a few more things to my list, the next two being closely related to Honesty.

My list went something like this:

Honesty

Trustworthy

Sincere

Caring

Communicator

Lover and Best Friend

Looking at the list, I believed I had followed it before, but apparently I let other things get in the way. I agreed that I would have to focus on me, on my needs and stop settling for less. I was worth so much more and did not have to put up with something or someone that made me feel uncomfortable or most importantly waved those darn red flags. From now on I would look at the red flags as they were meant to be, a warning or caution, and a green light to move on to something else.

I continued attending the workshops for a few months but then I stopped. Its not that I didn't enjoy the information being given, but it was becoming too repetitive for me, talking about the same things over and over again. I needed to move on to something more in my life, something more for me. I wanted to begin getting involved in things that would interest me more, like writing for instance. In the past, writing has been therapeutic for me. This was my chance to focus all of my attention on my thoughts and getting it down on paper in hopes that someday it would pay off. In addition I tried an advanced workshop given by the same facilitator of the singles meetings, but again, felt after a couple of sessions, that it was not for me.

The "singles" dinners were also something I enjoyed. I welcomed the opportunity to meet other people, female just as much as male. I was in no way looking to get involved in another relationship and I made that clear to the men that I met. I just wanted to create a new circle of friends. The men however were not interested in this and I was more or less told by one gentleman, that I should not be attending these functions if I wasn't looking to meet someone. I did date a couple of men from these socials but they never amounted to anything and never went any further than two dates. I was not ready for this and my biggest baggage was my ability to trust again. I felt much safer playing the friend role. Why is the "friend" word such a curse to men? Don't they understand that in order to build a relationship, you must first become friends? Anyway, lack of funds and some more discouragement had forced me to enjoy more of "me" time with just me and my thoughts.

I retreated back to being content playing a fun game of Slingo or Mah Jong on my computer and an occasional determination to pop all of the balloons in Poppit. It was nice to be quiet with myself and my thoughts and not think of anything else. I was learning to be comfortable with my life the way it was meant to be or so I thought.

Its now May 1st, 2005 and my life has changed in such a dramatic and incredible way. Before you continue reading, get yourself comfortable, grab a cup of coffee or tea, stretch or if the sun is still shining, go out and take a walk and catch a few rays. What I'm about to tell you is still unbelievable even to me.

Chapter Thirteen

My boyfriends back...

Donna Hanover wrote a book that I can relate to. Its titled "My Boyfriend's Back: True Stories of Rediscovering Love with a Long-Lost Sweetheart". This book didn't come out until a couple of weeks after yet another amazing journey of mine began.

Like I mentioned in the beginning of this book, I have always thought of my first love Tony. It wasn't an obsession or anything like that, but on occasion I would check the telephone book when a new edition came out, or, after joining Classmates. com, I would scan through the new members to see if Tony was listed there. He always held a special place in my heart, a vacancy that only my teenage memories of him could hold. In reality, he has been in my life forever. Like the words written all over the dust cover that protects my "Romeo and Juliet" album that he gave me way back then in high school, "Tony and Sandy 4 ever"! The *what ifs* have always continued to haunt me from time to time, but knowing that he was married and had a family, I had to put my feelings aside and be at ease with my decision years ago in 1972 when I told him it was over. I was not entirely happy with my choice after all that occurred in my marriage but I couldn't go back and change the past, and believing the phrase "what is meat to be" helped me to get past the guilt I felt over the years.

It was the 2nd week in January and what happened caught me completely off guard. I had a strange dream, one that drew concern to my mind and daily thoughts. The dream didn't make any sense at all, but Tony was in it looking so worn and sad.

When I woke up, I was so uncomfortable with what I saw. This was Tony, my Tony....what happened to him? This silly dream worried me for an entire week before I got up the nerve to search for him. I had to calm my crazy head and find out if he was ok. I searched and found his brother who got me in touch with his sister. The rest is history. You can ask anyone who knows me, but I have always believed in fate and that things happen for a reason. God drew me back to my roots as a young girl learning about love and the first love of my life, Tony

Like I said before, my boyfriends back and this whole unbelievable occurrence started with just a dream and a nagging determination to make sure he was fine. He is fine; as a matter of fact he is more wonderful than what I remember. We have reconnected in such an astonishing way, as if we never lost touch. We've rekindled old feelings for each other via phone, letters and cards. We've talked about the past, about our mistakes, of our regrets and have learned about the adult editions of Sandy and Tony. We've both changed in appearance, we've toughened up due to lifes hard earned lessons and we are both single and available. As I write this chapter, we have not yet seen each other because there is an obstacle, 3000 miles to be specific. Less than two weeks from today however, after 33 years, we will get to see each other again. Will we will be able to confirm this loving bond that has kept our hearts connected? Whether it be lasting friendship or something more, only time will tell and I can only fantasize and dream that all of this has happened because of fate, destiny or a prayer that has finally been answered.

Don't cheat now, don't skim to the last chapter to see what has become of the Tony Sandy saga. I don't want to think too far ahead of myself, but you can be sure my prayers have indeed gone into overtime.

Chapter Fourteen

So...what have I learned?

First and most importantly, pay attention to all of the red flags. Even if they are yellow or faint with a pinkish tone, question those damn flags. Don't defend what you don't know. Ask questions and if the answers don't suite you, move on.

While you are asking questions, listen to all that you are hearing. Don't feel that you are being nosey by asking why a person's marriage ended or if they've never been married, ask why?

Be wary of womanizing flirts or men who drink so much that they don't remember what they said the next day. Do they claim to be heroes in the military? Ask to see the Medal of Honor. Ask about their living arrangements. Living with good old Mom or homeless? And for goodness sake, if you been dating for years and you haven't been intimate with that person, its time to find out why?

Don't punish yourself for making mistakes but try not to repeat the same ones over and over again. Don't be so trusting, don't be so nice and play hard to get.

Do I sound bitter or burned? I'm not resentful of my experiences but figure if for nothing else, they have given me something to write about. And if I believe it has all happened for a reason, then the reason is so that I can pass on some of my wisdom, and witty experience with you.

There are also some great books out there that I wish I had read before. If I knew then what I know now...hey, that could be the title of my next book!

"Romantic Deception: The Six Signs He's Lying" by Sally Caldwell, Ph. D

"When Your Love is a Liar: Healing the Wounds of Deception and Betrayal" by Susan Forward and Donna Frazier

"101 Lies Men Tell Women and Why Women Believe Them" by Dory Hollander, Ph. D.

"Red Flags: How to Know When You're Dating a Loser" by Gary S. Aumiller

"Why Men Love Bitches: From Doormat to Dreamgirl – a Woman's Guide to Holding Her Own in a Relationship" by Sherry Argov

"He's Just Not That Into You: The No-Excuses Truth to Understanding Guys" by Greg Behrendt and Liz Tuccillo

"Be Honest-- You're Not That into Him Either: Raise Your Standards and Reach for the Love You Deserve" by Ian Kerner

All of these books have some valuable information along with the humor that you must hold on to while dating. For me and maybe others, dating was not that enjoyable, especially at my age. There are too many do's and don'ts and then at the same time, at this stage of life, what have you got to lose? Do you enjoy yourself to the fullest including the bed and breakfast weekends or do you play the Ms. Sophisticated Prima Donna and hope that the man you truly enjoy the company of understands that you are holding on to your self-dignified good-girl reputation for reasons of playing the game right? Maybe if I had read more of the books listed above, I would not have had my ego bashed or my heart bruised with the two specific game players I got involved with. Perhaps I would have had a lead in the game if I had read the rules first.

Along with the literature listed above, it's also good to get involved in community events geared specifically for singles. I mentioned previously that one I enjoyed most was the "Powers Singles" dinners. Sandra Powers who is the founder of this organization is amazing. She has a knack of making people feel comfortable among strangers and knows how to get communication going and get everyone involved. Unfortunately, unless you live in the New York area, you cannot take advantage of this opportunity, but if you do, be sure to check out her website first at http://www.powerssingles.com/ or email her at Powerssingles@aol.com . Trust me, you won't go away feeling dismayed, but instead feel that you have made some new friends and maybe meet someone significant at that.

Another group that I spoke of earlier was The Human Development Company that was founded by Stefan Deutcsh. It was beneficial to me in that I learned more about myself and my needs and why I kept repeating the same pattern over and over again in my life. It seems we more or less condition ourselves to just *settle* for things or in this case, people as they come into our lives. In Stefan's training, we are taught to look for specific qualities or characteristics that make us happy. All of this made perfect sense, unfortunately not all of us have the patience or self respect to focus entirely on ourselves and our needs. If we all did this, the world might be a better place. There would be less frustration, less anger and perhaps less divorces if people would take the time to learn about themselves before selecting and getting attached to their companions. If you are interested in joining Stefan's self-help groups, you can reach him at info @thehumandevelopmentcompany.com or check out his new dating website, http://www.justsayyestolove.com/.

There are so many other ideal opportunities out there today to meet that special someone. Though I myself have never tried it, there is a growing population in attending events called "Speed Dating". The premise of it is to spend several minutes questioning or interviewing potential or available singles in a precise age bracket. It sounds like a good idea, but for myself, I would need much more than several minutes to find out if there is a possibility that I may be interested in someone and he in me. I suppose if you go in with the attitude that you are there for fun and have no expectations, then it could be a rewarding experience.

I've heard that Singles Cruises are also fun, though if you are my age and don't mind being with a younger crowd, then you might be able to fit yourself in without feeling as though you are the chaperone of the Love Boat.

The key is patience, making yourself available and finding the right chance to search for and meet Mr. or Ms. Right. Only one may be suitable for you depending on the circumstances involved. What is good for one person may not always be good for someone else. Are you looking for fun and adventure or are you looking for a serious long-term relationship and possibly marriage?

Whatever the case may be, it's advisable to try different things before you give up completely, even if it means turning back the hour glass or listening to your dreams. Follow your instincts with caution and remember past mistakes before plunging in head first.

Chapter Fifteen

Ok, we are adult's here....so can we talk?

I wish there was a dating guide for all ages, for all situations, that would tell you explicitly what you can or cannot, or should or should not do...sort of like a dictionary, thesaurus or encyclopedia. So many times I would say the wrong thing to avoid the chance of hurting another's feelings or the uncomfortable possibility that I would need to explain myself further. I admit I was not good at being completely honest when it came to telling my date exactly what I felt about him. I would find myself agreeing heartily with every conversation made and then when I sensed the wrong impression was being made on my part, I would panic and the defensive side of Sandy would suddenly appear.

My first experience with this was when I met one of my first Joes at Starbucks. I felt terrible that I was judging this man on appearance and not on the former conversations we had before our meeting. So instead of telling him nicely that I felt no attraction to him, I put my foot in my mouth by telling him we should meet again. What on earth would possess me to get myself in deeper when I knew damn well how I felt? And of course I took the chickens way out by ignoring his emails. How rude! If this type of action was done to me, I know I would be hurt and just as annoyed. He was angry of course, and I really didn't blame him.

Another time, remembering my mistake in the past, I did try to be honest with someone even though, yes, I did take the wimpy way out by sending him an email. But nevertheless, I did let him know and then never heard from him again even when I suggested in my email that we be friends. What did I do wrong? Its not like I let the situation drag on for days or weeks, in fact I informed him immediately after our date. I apologized in my message and tried letting him know it wasn't him at all but that I felt there were no common interests between us. I was a bit insulted that he never responded but I tried to see it from his side and I suppose his male ego was hurt.

So the bottom line is you are damned if you do and damned if you don't. We cant please all of the people all of the time.

And what about the courtesy of returning phone calls? One gentleman for instance I found very nice even though I didn't feel any attraction to. I really thought if nothing else, we could become good friends. His company was enjoyable, he was distinguished and seemingly intelligent and some of the things we spoke of I found very intriguing. Then one weekend, on a Saturday, I was to meet him at a ballpark but woke up that morning feeling extremely ill. Knowing this was an outdoor event and I would be sitting in the sun or on bleachers, I decided I would not be the best company. I tried calling him and had no choice but to leave a message on his answering machine. When I didn't hear from him, I tried his cell phone and then tried his home again and again leaving several messages hoping I would catch him in time so he wouldn't think I stood him up. I never received a return call nor did I ever hear from him again. I suppose that was his way of telling me he was not interested in me, but now the shoe was on the other foot and I was feeling somewhat rejected. Why couldn't he just come right out and say what he felt instead of leaving me hanging, wondering what I did wrong or for that matter if he was dead or alive?

Is it wrong to allow a friendship to develop? Another situation developed where I had met another very nice man. We seemed to have things in common and shared our stories and our experiences with each other and it was all very comfortable or so I thought. We had coffee once or twice and met a couple of times after that, strictly on a friend to friend basis. Then as quickly or slowly in this case, that our friendship started, I never heard from him again. He just poofed out of existence. I still wonder if I said or did something to scare him away. If he ever reads this, I would like to extend my apologies, only because I did respect him as a friend and would have hoped he felt the same.

Here we are again, damned if we do and damned if we don't.

Now let's turn to the other side of the coin. How do we act when we *are* attracted to someone? Do we let them know immediately, do we hide it, play hard to get and hope for the chase or let it go gradually and risk the chance of losing the relationship that could have been? Then there is the problem of getting too deeply involved with someone. Do we act on our instincts or do we act like teenagers and remember what Mother or Father told us or what our upbringing prohibits us from expressing to another human being, in this case, the opposite sex? In simpler terms and straight out, when is it okay to engage in sex? At my age, I would want to believe its okay but then there is always that taboo feeling of guilt from our childhood or the fear that the engagement is labeling us as a tramp or slut.

In my day...is my age showing yet? ... any girl who did "*it*" was classified as a tramp unless of course you were going steady with that one guy, it was considered acceptable. But if you were dating several guys...oh my...watch out! Like when a dog is in heat, when the word got out, every guy in school and even in other school districts would come running to see who this tramp was and if she really did what the bathroom walls claimed she did. How unfair life is? It was and still is fine when men go to first or second base but for the female gender, its slander punishable by stoning.

So that brings me back to my first objective on this topic. When is it okay? And how does it look to the man? What are his thoughts? What does he think of her? Does he think less of her if she does *it*, or does he respect her as a human being with feelings and understand that she has desires just like he does?

From my own experience, once the act is engaged in, it can sometimes be hard to decipher what the true intent was. I know we are adults, but our hearts react the same way as that teenage girl who has a crush on the boy next door or the boy who sits behind her in class and pulls her hair and taunts her with tease. When a man makes goo goo eyes at you, one that you may find attractive, your brain goes into a blank state of mind. You can't think straight or make rational decisions and before you know it, he's got you and you are falling into that abyss of love. I know life is all about taking chances and sometimes we do have to take that step or be forever regretful, but it can also hurt like hell when it doesn't work out. At this age or period of my life, I'm too old for broken hearts. Been there, done that and I'm not going back there again!

So this is where my dating ends and my new life begins. It could either be spent alone without that man beside me 24/7, without the pain and anger that occasionally goes along with a relationship or be satisfied knowing I am surrounded by friends, male and female to fill that void I had hoped to seal up.

This is not to say that life cannot be appreciated and happy as a single middle-aged adult, but in my own personal situation, I do long for the warmth and comfort you feel when there is that special person going along for the ride with you. Life for me is much better when you can share your day to day, moment to moment existence. Just knowing that there is someone to listen to your thoughts, whether they are intelligent or nonsensical and silly. Laughter and fun along with the tears and sadness are bearable when it done jointly.

Chapter Sixteen

My advice...

I'm no Ann Landers, Doctor Ruth, Doctor Phil, Oprah or expert in the field of dating but I do have some advice to single woman, and also to the men out there looking for their Cinderella who fits into that glass slipper. If you are serious about finding your partner in life and not out for the fun of it, then stop playing the game. Clean up your act before you begin your quest.

Get over your last loves. Make sure the last girlfriend or boyfriend is totally out of the picture before you move on to another heart. If it is an ex-spouse, be sure that your feelings of resentment, betrayal, anger or even continued feelings of love are behind you so that you don't drag the baggage around with you from table to table. I'm just as guilty of this, so it is easier said than done. What date really wants to hear about your past relationship problems? Unless you are old pals, they really aren't interested and if they aren't getting paid an hourly wage for it, they don't want to listen to you cry over the past.

If needed, get into therapy before your next pursuit or adventure. It's good to get a trained persons view of the situation so that you can examine your movements and choices that have been made in the past. In therapy, I found some very interesting things about myself, some I'm not too proud of but at least I see now why I do the things I do. Sometimes I realize after the fact and after the damage is done, but I'm learning to see the signs before hand. Because I am an enabler, I go out of my way to do things for others or the ones I love in order to keep life running smoothly. I hate confrontation and will go to any means to avoid it even if it means getting my feelings hurt. When the bomb drops, I take the blame and make up excuses for the other person. I still find myself doing this subconsciously. I just wish there was a way I could make my subconscious alert me like an alarm clock or timer.

When you are out on your date, be yourself. Don't pretend to be someone you are not. It's nice to talk about children or grandchildren if you have any, talk about your pets, about trips you may have taken, sometimes it's even nice to discuss your job as long as it doesn't involve politics. Chat about books you've read, movies you've seen or television shows you watch. Hobbies or Sports can be another conversation opener as long as you don't go overboard describing in detail every sport you play, every team you watch or every color and intricate stitch you've put into the quilt you made last Fall. Watch for facial expressions, look at the other person's eyes, and take notice of the way they move when they speak. These things, however silly they may seem, give you an idea of the personality and character of this possible Jane or Joe. Be open and never judgmental, listen intently and repeat things they have said. This awareness lets the other person know you are interested.

Chapter Seventeen

and about those damn red flags...

One final thought before I bring my story to an end... beware of those damn red flags and listen to your friends and family if they try to make you aware of the red signs you are not seeing. If it means saving you some precious time, and if you missed the ones I spoke of before, let me share my experienced red flags with you once more.

If your date continuously talks about or shows anger towards his ex-wife, then move on girlfriend. I know I have done this too, so I shouldn't pass too much judgment on this one, but how many times can you listen to him complain about his ex? Could it be that he is still hung up on her? Perhaps there is more to this situation then the daily inquiry about the kids or the support check, sharing the holidays or the same house. Move on sister girlfriend, move on!

Or how about that first date... he drives to your door to pick you up, honks the horn or calls you on the cell to let you know he's waiting outside? What happened to chivalry? I know I may be too old for you to impress my mother, but come on buddy? And while you are at it, would you mind picking up the trash in your car. A car deodorizer might help too.

And that reminds me of the gentleman that brings you to his house for some quiet music, maybe a drink and a roaring fire on a cold night. First and utmost, please please please, get a housecleaner before this thought ever enters your mind. No woman wants to be fearful of sitting on something that moves or for that matter, stepping on something that crunches as she walks across the floor. And instead of aiming your kitchen sink faucet sprayer at the fireplace to extinguish the flame, how about visiting the local home improvement center or hardware store like Sears, Home Depot or Lowes? Amazing as it may seem, but technology has certainly advanced over the years and I hear they now have handy fireplace tools for situations like this.

For that date that is head over heals for you from the get go and is trying so hard to impress you with all that he can do for you, all that he can be for you and that includes adjusting his height, weight and age...I don't know what to say to you. I know exactly how you feel. I've been there so many times myself. We want to be exactly who and what that other person is looking for but you know what?...if there is no chemistry from the beginning, then I truly don't think it will develop over time. For every man or woman out there, there is definitely a match for you somewhere. Hang in there sweetie.

For big red flag number one, I admit I was intrigued and extremely vulnerable. You fought in the war, saved people from burning buildings, attended and earned a MBA from an accredited college...get off your horse and ride the train like the rest of the world. We know who you want to be, we understand that you would have liked to accomplish more in your life, but who you are now is much more important compared to what you could have been. I'm sure there is a wonderful person in that scrambled mind of yours, but you have issues sir, and you need to take care of them before you continue to drag other people down with you.

Hugh blinking red flag with a siren blaring....you may have thought you were giving me the world, enticing me with the things money can buy and again, I was caught up in your game of lies and deceit. What hurt the most was the fact that you knew of my past and my baggage and hang-ups about dishonesty. To all of you women out there....if the ex-girlfriends picture is on the dresser, turn around and walk away. Let me rephrase that... run as quickly as you can and don't look back. This particular fling was just an alcoholic event that turned into a five month hangover. It was fun to have a drinking buddy but that's all it should have been. I take total responsibility here and all I can say now is I hope the girlfriend on the dresser has tamed the wild boy.

Chapter Eighteen

My first love, my last love...

The day is Sunday, November 20th of the year 2005. I sit here at my computer finalizing my thoughts and my situation. I am presently residing in California, far away from the life I have lived for the past 50 years. I am surrounded by the West coast sun most of the time and enveloped in something I have dreamt about but never actually thought would ever in my wildest dreams take place. My dream, my fairy tale ending, my prince charming, my search for the Average Joe has come to an end. I am with Tony, my first love and now my last love.

After reconnecting with Tony back in January and then visiting with him in May, I decided to take a chance with the new road set before me. When we met for the first time in 33 years at the airport, I knew immediately what I had lost or gave up so many years before. I didn't have to think twice or evaluate what my heart was telling me. When I looked into his eyes, I saw my Tony, the boy I grew up with, the boy I learned about love with, the boy whose heart I broke when I moved out of town and our lives drifted apart. If I could take back the pain and the decision I made then, I would. If only I could have told him then what I wanted or how I felt, let him know what was going on in my head, maybe we would never have been apart. But for whatever reason or whatever Gods plan was for us, we both gained knowledge and beautiful gifts in the form of children that we can both be proud of jointly with our ex-spouses. We look at our children and see our accomplishment, our greatest asset to society and pray that they don't repeat the same mistakes we have.

With our children still being our priority, we now also have each other to focus and learn from all over again. We have reawakened our youth and rekindled the love we both had at the very young age of 13 through 18 years old and I can tell you honestly and from my heart, it is the most glorious feeling I have felt in a very very long time. Like the line from my favorite movie, "There's no place like home" or the saying, "You don't know what you had until you don't have it anymore", what we had so many years ago is amazingly still alive. I have learned over the past few months that there really is no place like home, that the grass is not always greener on the other side and what I had then took me 33 years to realize was the best thing that ever happened in my life, besides the birth of my children.

Everyday I wake up and can't help but stare at the older version of my Tony and thank God for this wonder that has occurred in our lives. I see only green lights on this road and listen to my heart and feel the lump that forms in my throat each time I remember that day in the airport back in May. My Tony... waiting nervously at the bottom of the escalator with a rose in his hand for his high school sweetheart not knowing if she will embrace him with open arms or turn and run the other way. Me... wondering if he notices that I'm not the thin young girl I used to be or if he sees the grey hairs that I missed when I did my late night hair coloring job the night before. In the weeks that followed, we both felt the love that we've always felt for each other and dreaded the day that I had to head back home to New York.

Now it's November in California, and yes, it is a marvel that I am here and that my life and his has changed in such a dramatic way. Like any other couple, we both have had our moments of frustration and some anger with each other, but have come to realize that even though we knew each other as kids, there is so much more to catch up on and learn all over again. This miracle may have happened overnight but our old/

new relationship needs to be nurtured with patience, time and understanding.

I feel as though I have somehow gone back to my roots, the beginning, where I began, where I started to grow and learn about life, with its heartaches and rewards. I've reconnected with that special person who has all of the qualities I ever wanted in a person. I have found honesty and sincerity and someone who is trustworthy and caring. He is a great communicator; he is my lover and my best friend. I have someone who adores me and loves me for who I am, who wants to share life and the daily thoughts that accompany it, who will climb the highest mountain and cross the deepest sea... I won't go into a Diana Ross song and dance here, but why did it take me all of my life to see that what I wanted most, was there from the start? How unfortunate for us both that we had to go through a lifetime to find each other again.

Chapter Nineteen

life is truly beautiful...

I don't want to continuously bore you with my sour experiences of past loves gone bad and all of the questions looking for answers, so I suppose I can finally bring my journey and this phase of my life, the life of the single middle aged woman to an end. Joyfully, my search for that Average Joe has ended. It is a year now since I had that weird dream that sent me searching for Tony and I can confidently say that I have found my match, hooked with my soul mate and can think now of the possibilities that are in store for us in the near future. My life is on such a high now that I feel somewhat guilty telling people how happy I am. Everything is so much more enjoyable, from getting up in the morning to my commute home each night. I do undoubtedly, carry that shadow of blame knowing that my children are still in New York, thrown into an independence that perhaps they were not prepared for but I also spend each day thinking of my new life and at times, selfishly nothing else. All I want to do now is create plans for a future and make-up for the time I missed with Tony. I don't care about the house with the white picket fence and goal for the American dream anymore. I don't care about the luxuries we sometimes dream about or the vacation destinies I have told myself to take before I die, nor do I daydream of winning the big lottery. Cloudy days or unseasonable cool temperatures have no effect on my moods any longer, if anything, I take pleasure in listening and seeing all that I am experiencing in my life now. I have even found myself coping with the bumper to bumper traffic that has become a part of my daily life commuting on the California freeway. My life seems to have moved into the slow lane with each day being an extraordinary gift that I am learning to enjoy and not take for granted. I am so deeply in love and so grateful for the opportunity set before me…and I am trying to take caution not to screw it up. I've been given a miraculous conclusion for my story, one so totally unexpected. I've made many wrong choices in the past and now for the first time, the choice I've made feels so unbelievably right. Tony and I have been handed a 2nd chance at love, a love that we are both determined not to lose again.

I hope that all of the Average Janes and all of the Average Joes everywhere can one day end their search and come across the chance to find true love and happiness. Don't give up if you haven't reached that plateau. It can happen when you least expect it, when you aren't looking and then like magic, in the blink of an eye, someone is there to fill the vacancy and your life suddenly feels like it is transcending.

That's how it was for me, as if I was uplifted or on a ride that I didn't want to end. My life, which I felt was incomplete, is now full to the max. Now I can stand back and observe it all and enjoy the contentment it brings and the new view from a slightly different angle. I never thought this day would come, never believed my life could turn out this way, in simpler terms… *life is truly beautiful!*

one more acknowledgement before I go…

I wanted to update my acknowledgement in the beginning of this book, but decided this person needed a more personable one of his own.

This is for Tony, my first love, the love my mother said was just puppy love, the love I thought I would in time forget, the love that never left my heart. I love you for never forgetting me and for being a part of my life even when you didn't know it. I thank you for not dismissing the letter you received back in January, for going with your heart and your intuition and giving 2nd chances a try. I appreciate and respect your honesty with me from the beginning, your truthful and caring ways and for being my best friend. I thank you for loving me for me and not expecting me to be someone I am not. I love you for who you are and believe me when I say I don't need or want anything more. You have made me the happiest woman in the world and no one or anything can bring our new journey to an end.

This time is for us, lets take what God has meant for us to enjoy...together.

My love is yours forever,
Sandy

Sandy
&
Tony
4 ever!